C. F Rice

Poems, Translations and Hymns

C. F Rice

Poems, Translations and Hymns

ISBN/EAN: 9783337241919

Printed in Europe, USA, Canada, Australia, Japan

Cover: Foto ©Thomas Meinert / pixelio.de

More available books at **www.hansebooks.com**

POEMS

TRANSLATIONS

AND

HYMNS

BY

C. F. RICE

"'These, these are but the Songs they sing';
They are the Singer's life!"

𝔇𝔲𝔟𝔩𝔦𝔫

HODGES, FIGGIS, AND CO.

1888

DUBLIN:
PRINTED AT THE UNIVERSITY-PRESS,
BY PONSONBY AND WELDRICK.

Contents.

SONNETS IN MEMORIAM.

	Page.
SALOME'S PRAYER, ...	3
THE AMARANTHS—I., . . .	4
,, II., . . .	4
,, III.,	5
EXOTICS, ...	5
LIFE'S MEASURE, ...	6
IN MEMORIAM, R. C. TRENCH, . .	6
IN MEMORIAM, A. H. MACKONOCHIE, . .	7

SONNETS.

THE CRUCIBLE, . .	8
PEARLS, . . .	9
"THEN SHALL WE KNOW," . . .	9
SUGGESTED BY MÜLLERS'S HOLY FAMILY, . .	10
THE BIRD AT DAWN, .	10

CONTENTS.

	Page.
THE RECEDING SHIP,	11
UNHEARD MUSIC,	11
AN EARLY LESSON,	12
FADED FLOWERS,	12
"ALL WORKS OF GOD ARE GOOD,"	13
FAILING SIGHT,	13
THE MOON,	14
THE DOVE AT THE LATTICE,	14
A PENITENT,	15
DEVELOPMENT,	15
MATERNAL JOY,	16
CATHEDRAL WINDOWS,	16
"HIMSELF HE CANNOT SAVE!"	17
FLIGHT,	17
PROPHETS OF DESPAIR,	18
AN APPEAL,	18
FAITH'S TRIAL—I.,	19
,, II.,	19
,, III.,	20
,, IV.,	20
,, V.,	21
FOLDED WINGS,	21
TO SOME MODERN POETS,	22

POEMS.

SEAGULLS,	23
BEREAVEMENT,	25
THE SPARROW'S FLIGHT,	27
LOVE'S DECISION,	29
A LAMENT—PRELUDE AND SONG,	32

CONTENTS.

	Page
LONDON,	34
YE FAERIE ROSE,	38
THE UNKNOWN FUTURE,	39
IN MEMORIAM, SIR E. LANDSEER,	41
LOVE'S SEASONS,	43
A BIRCH TREE IN GLYNSOUTHWELL,	45
THE BIRCH TREE IN WINTER,	46
IN MEMORIAM, G. W. F. REICHEL,	48
UNCONSCIOUS HAPPINESS,	50
"ONCE OVER ALL,"	50
THE ASCENT OF MOUNT HOR,	53
TO THE SOUTH WIND,	56
FADED HEATHER,	57
KILLED BY ACCIDENT,	60
FROM THE PROSE OF SHAFTESBURY,	63
SLEEP,	64
TO C. E. R.,	66

TRANSLATIONS.

WAITING,	67
A FUNERAL,	68
THE DUTY OF MAN,	69
LINES WRITTEN IN A RONSARD,	69
THE LITTLE SHROUD,	70
"TEMPUS FUGIT,"	71
A LAST WISH,	71
LISTEN, MADELAINE.	72
HER NAME,	74
UNIVERSAL LIBERTY,	75
THE SAW-MILL.	77

CONTENTS.

	Page.
THE FAY, . .	78
MOSES ON THE NILE,	79
SUMMER RAIN, . .	82
THE YOUNG MOTHER, . .	85

HYMNS.

FOR THE DAY OF INTERCESSION FOR MISSIONS, . .	87
FOR A VIGIL, ...	89
DEDICATION OF A CHURCH, ...	90
SURSUM CORDA, ...	91
FOR EASTER EVE, ...	92
THANKSGIVING FOR DELIVERANCE FROM SICKNESS,	93
HARVEST HYMN, ...	95

Dedicated

TO THE MEMORY OF

CECIL AND NORA.

GEN. xliii. 14.

TWO children, by my tear-dimmed vision seen,
    Roam hand in hand the fields of Paradise;
And by the soft light in their kindred eyes,
The sunny locks with scarce a shade between,
The nostril fine, and fair broad brow serene,
I know them linked by sweet fraternal ties—
I know the babes, whose tender memory lies
In my bereaved heart for ever green.
Yet tho' bereaved, shall I mourn that they
For evermore escape the pain and woe
Shared by the happiest in this world below?
Christ, who didst once take babes upon Thy knee,
Grant me both faith and patience, Lord, I pray,
Meekly to suffer mine to go to Thee.

May 17th, 1885.

Motherhood.

TO C. C. R.

O VANISHED year, in memory live!
    Hallowed and gladdened, awed and blest,
By the first thrill of mother's love,
    Its happy care, its sweet unrest:

Its thousand hopes, that fain would raise
    The future's never-lifted veil;
Its thousand fears, that stronger still
    Would trembling see those hopes prevail.

O vanished year, in memory live!
    Long in its dim cells lingering;
For such a bright and joy-fraught hour
    No future year may ever bring

As that which told my weary brain
    That pain was past, that there had come
A little treasure to my heart,
    A little sunbeam to my home,

Which real made what long had been
    But a sweet picture, fancy-limned,
That ever fair and fairer grew,
    Till its light outlines, tear-bedimmed,

Faded and past—which, O my child!
    Gave thy young life to me to tend,
And gave me, in thy tiny form,
    To see mine own unite and blend

With one which to thine infant face
    Full many a look and smile imparts,
Thou little sweet result of love
    That fills and floods my heart of hearts!

O surely, if from mortal lips
    One prayer may pure and sinless be,
'Tis that which for her infant breathed
    First bends a new-made Mother's knee.

And, rising from her inmost heart,
    To the Great Parent throned above,
Would ask, for His most precious gift,
    The highest blessing of His Love:

Would ask, as I, my Babe, for thee,
    (Grant Thou my prayer, Most Good, Most Wise),
That life's sweet flower which blossoms here
    May bloom for aye in Paradise.

1870.

SONNETS IN MEMORIAM.

Salome's Prayer.

FOND Mother, type of many a mother now,
   Well may I picture her with looks intent
And eager steps in loving hurry bent
Towards His feet, where none in vain might bow:
I see the gracious pity on His brow,
As, answering the prayer in which she spent
Her heart's desire, He gave His strange consent
To bless her sons, altho' He spake not how.
I, like Salome, prayed, my child, for thee,
With loftiest hopes, and all as little dreamed
How in His wisdom God would answer me:
Yet may I hope my prayer fulfilled to see,
Where that sweet face, which here an angel's seemed,
Shall shine with a celestial purity

February 15th, 1880.

The Amaranths.

I.

WE through the garden roved, my boy and I,
  Seeking for flowers that had escaped the wreck
Wrought by autumnal storms, wherewith to deck,
One happy festal day, God's Sanctuary:
Then did the child a bed of amaranths spy,
And eager clutched their buds: I sought to check
His rifling hand, willing that on the neck
Of the dead year one fadeless wreath should lie.
But then, methought, these buds will never blow
Beneath dark skies, and so I bade the boy
Gather at his sweet will: the buds I found
Months afterwards, fresh as when long ago
The small hand plucked them; but the child, my joy,
My amaranth flower, sleeps in the churchyard ground.

II.

PERCHANCE the King who all the future sees,
And knows what clouds above His garden brood,
Bade Death's dark angel pluck my opening bud.
Perchance He knew it might nor bear the breeze
Which shakes to sturdier strength the forest trees:
That its soft petals 'neath embraces rude
Would withered fall; for, framed in tender mood,
A chilly blast its very soul would freeze.
So the frail form lies in that sanctuary,
Where all sweet things are stored—our mother earth—
To slumber there whence first it took its birth:
But ah! not there the vital spirit lies,
That winged a passage fetterless and free
Into God's angel-guarded Paradise.

III.

And these shall meet again; a colour fair
Shall flush the cheek anew, while to the eye
The soul returns to take the sovereignty
Lost for a little while. Death did not dare
To bid the free immortal Spirit share
The body's strange decay: it could not die;
No earth might cover that, no marble lie
In cold repression on its essence rare.
And, while the amaranths wear to day the bloom
They had when shut from sight, the opening tomb
Shall give the flower I yielded grudgingly
In more than pristine beauty back to me:
Through God's great alchemy, in darkness wrought,
In glory unrevealed, past human thought.

June, 1884.

Exotics.

It was thy birthday, and I gathered flowers
  To dress thy grave: meanwhile the breeze of May
Tossed the light leaves in its audacious play,
And caught and bent the blossoms of her bowers.
Then suddenly one of Spring's swift brief showers
Athwart the sunbeams flashed its diamond spray,
And drove me where, from hardier flowers away,
Fair, frail exotics pass their sheltered hours.
How great the change! Without the wind, the rain,
Within a tropic warmth, a fragrant air,
Then o'er my spirit sweetest comfort stole:
I thought of thee, my flower, 'soul of my soul,'
Safe-housed, and by the Heavenly Gardener's care
Protected till thou greet mine eyes again.

May 17th, 1884.

Life's Measure.

LIFE is not told by years! I had a child
  Whose slender span was but six summers long :
His bud of life that burst to mid-May's song
Fell blighted soon 'midst wintry tempests wild ;
Yet when I think upon him, undefiled,
His ways, looks, words, his spirit soft, yet strong,
More tender recollections round me throng
Than many a life of threescore years could yield.
Ah me! too truly does a poet sing,
'Oh! sir, the good die first' ; yet, though we ring
Their early knell, we will not deem their fate
Unhappy; they but quit earth's dark estate
To live in peace, and memory's light, and prove
That life is measured less by time than love.

January, 1885.

In Memoriam.
R. C. TRENCH.

FAREWELL: thou Scholar, Poet, Priest,—and Saint.
  When all is said, the last and highest style
Befits thee best, thou Spirit without guile.
Soon to thy scholar's mind without restraint
Truth shall unlock her stores : scenes none might paint
Delight thy poet's eye : a little while,
And thou, a priest within no earthly pile,
Shalt serve where worship may not fail nor faint.
And oh! thy saintly soul, which here below
Seemed half in heaven to live : what shall it know?
Where change, nor pain, nor sorrow may betide,
To all beloved and lost for aye restored,
Clothed in the likeness of its living Lord,
It shall awake and shall be satisfied!

April, 1886.

In Memoriam.

A. H. MACKONOCHIE.*

TRUE Knight of God! we hold it not unmeet
    That thou shouldst face the inevitable foe,
With his still weapons armed, frost, mist, and snow,
Upon the lonely heights, and so complete
A valorous life that never owned defeat.
Unwise at times thou seem'dst, yet few may know
How much for conscience' sake thou didst forego;
How brave thy toil in study, church, and street.
And it had been, O Knight of dauntless heart,
To thee, perchance, a hardier, wearier part,
To wait death creeping slow in rear of age,
Than 'gainst his might one short sharp strife to wage,
Then sink unconquered, by his very hand
Who struck, admitted to the deathless land.

    December, 1887.

---

* Vicar of S. Alban's, Holborn, who perished in a mountain snowstorm in Scotland.

SONNETS.

"All things are double."—BACON.

The Crucible.

MAL. iii. 2, 3.

INTO the crucible his precious ore
   With careful hand the skilled refiner throws.
So dull, so dark the rugged metal shows
That one might trample it, nor deem it more
Than the cheap clay upon earth's common floor.
Yet the refiner as the white heat glows
Keeps keenest watch, nor rests until he knows
His own face mirrored in a glittering store.
God sits as a refiner: He will cast
The nature rich with undiscovered gold
Into His crucible on sorrow's fire,
Then patient wait, until at last, at last,
His Image there, freed from earth's dimming mould,
Shine ever clearer as the flames mount higher.

November, 1881.

Pearls.

THE mussel clingeth to its native rock,
    And closely clingeth, yet the furious sea
Will sometimes wrench it thence all suddenly,
With that rude might which doth all forces mock:
Then 'neath its armour, riven by the shock,
Fair silver drops of perfect symmetry
Spring forth to heal the wounded panoply,
And the small shell with priceless pearls to stock.
So sometimes souls, in earth's frail mansions housed,
Dashed on the shoals of sin by storms of life,
Lie spent and shattered in the unequal strife.
Yet happy they, if by their sufferings roused,
Bright tears of love and penitence flow down,
On earth to heal, in Heaven to light a crown.

"Then shall we know, even as also we are known."

AND this great thing shall be! O blessed truth!
    Amidst life's thousand vague perplexities—
Amidst the thronging hopes and fears that rise
In childhood's fancy, the hot heart of youth,
Yea, in the mind of manhood, which in sooth
For knowledge with the saddest yearning cries,
This promise comes to silence scoffing lies,
To calm youth's restlessness, soothe age's ruth.
'As we are known' God knows us perfectly:
No earth-born mists may hide His sons from Him,
And, as a Father, pitying his own child,
Bewildered often, oftener yet beguiled,
He guides us, till with sense no longer dim,
We solve in Heaven's full light life's mystery.

Suggested by Muller's Holy Family.

SHRINES set within a shrine, again enshrined
    Within the Virgin Mother's fond embrace,
Are those deep infant eyes which seek her face,
So flower-like fair, above their light declined.
How sweet her smile maternal, all refined
By reverent wonder at the mystic grace,
The power in weakness, she may dimly trace
The lineaments of infancy behind.
Now and for ever upon God's right hand
Is one sole seat of royal dignity,
Yet, if another might unchallenged stand
The splendours of the great white Throne anigh,
'Twere hers, who on her maiden bosom bore
That Babe whom Seraphim stooped to adore.

The Bird at Dawn.

WHEN in the latest watches of the night,
    Upon my couch, all unrefreshed, I turn,
Mine ears, through silence sensitive, discern
The bird's first whisper, tremulous and slight,
Yet musical, with an untold delight.
Then doth my spirit, sadly sighing, yearn
The secret of that happiness to learn
Which seems to fill his little being quite.
Why does he spring to meet the new-born day,
With wing so buoyant and with voice so gay,
While man, unhappy, fain would sleep for aye?
This truth from nature, O sad heart, receive,
Thy very misery then shall comfort give:
The earthly only earth may satisfy.

The Receding Ship.

WE watch the fair ship speed across the bay,
　　Then out into the offing, and we gaze,
While sight may strain its willing strength, to trace
Her white sails, ever lessening, until they
Shrink to a speck upon the horizon grey:
A moment more—her mast's tip only stays
To show where still she lives, a point in space,
Then 'neath the round world's curve she sinks away.
How smooth her flight! in one brief hour her sail
Has swept the slope that proves our earth a sphere!
Now mark the traveller wind by hill and dale,
Pacing with weary step paths long and drear:
Like this—life's journey is, to finite men;
Like that—its memory will be, when, ah! when?

　　Bray, August, 1886.

Unheard Music.

WHEN the gay Spring, alike by cot and grange,
　　And where man dwells not, thro' the wild bird's throat
Tells her glad tale in many a tuneful note,
Sweet voices with tumultuous interchange,
Now shrill, now low, the diapason range:
But in their midst some rapturous anthems float
Too high for man's dull sense, the blue remote
Receives to its pure heights that music strange.
So oft the poet's soul must sing alone
For listeners not of earth; his mystic tone
Has compass for the common ear too high:
Man heeds him not, his audience room the sky,
Its silence and its space: his songs require
A scope as boundless as his heart's desire.

An Early Lesson.

ONE day my boy brought me a gaudy flower
    That charmed his childish taste, and deemed that mine
Would find delight in one so large and fine;
And, in return, he asked me to restore
Fair flowers, an offering of the day before:
In his young memory's yet unsullied shrine
They lived as bright as when his hand did twine
Their dewy wreath in the fresh morning hour.
I brought the blossoms—o'er the little face
Passed a quick change, for in a glance he learned
The lesson that is surely taught to all:
Even that Time, tho' slow his stealthy pace
Seem to our youth, is never backward turned,
But, 'neath his scythe, bids every beauty fall.

Faded Flowers.

WITH hurried hand within a vase I placed
    Fresh gathered flowers, and left them there to bloom,
And deemed that thro' long hours my sunless room
Would by their sweetness and their light be graced:
I came again, and petals dank defaced
My garland gay, and dulled its sweet perfume:
Close to the water—not within—their doom
To die of thirst thro' my unheeding haste.
So oft, alas! we bear these souls of ours
In careless mood where living fountains spring,
Lift to their lips the very Wine of Heaven,
Yet find them unrefreshèd as the flowers:
Nor strength renewed, nor fragance thence they bring,
For these, not sought in earnest, are not given.

Whitsun Day, 1885.

"All Works of God are good."

WITHIN the weary street sand, clay, and soot,
  To clog men's steps in compound foul combine,
But let great Nature separate, refine,
And with her touch miraculous transmute,
And each unto its noblest purpose put:
Amidst the sand the changeful opals shine;
From the rude clay springs porcelain fair and fine;
From refuse smoke the diamond's glories shoot.
All works of God are good: do not despise
A brother's being, nor debase thine own.
Take courage! from the dust of earth arise!
Not yet God's purposes in thee are shown:
O thwart not thou thy Maker's gracious plan
When in His Image He created man.

Failing Sight.

GREAT Nature rules that as time rolleth on
  The tints and shapes of beauties seen anear
Fade to our fading eyes. The rose must wear
For us a paler robe, her petals wan
A fainter outline show than that which shone
On our young gaze; yet is the distance clear,
And its blue hills are more than ever dear,
For the vague dread that childhood knew is gone.
So with the spirit's vision dealeth time;
The present paleth, but the future hour
Shines on the enfranchised sight with fullest power;
The shades mysterious clothing hills untrod
Appal not him whose aged sense sublime
Discerns beneath the hidden things of God.

The Moon.

DOGGING Earth's steps, alike by night and day,
    Moves that pale prophetess, a wasted world:
For evermore have light and life been hurled
From her cold brow, which feeleth not the ray
That warms our happier earth: about her stray
Fair fleecy clouds, now lightly streaked and curled,
Cradling her desolation, now unfurled,
Floating like flags above a funeral way.
O race of men, boasting with finite pride
Your conquests over Nature: as ye smile,
She moveth to her triumph all the while:
And those great forces ye are weak to guide
Will leave at last this scene of all your skill
Like that prophetic Moon—bare, cold, and still.

The Dove at the Lattice.
A TRUE INCIDENT.

SADLY returned we from the Sacred Feast
    One holy morn, for life seemed fraught with gloom;
The times were cruel: spent was summer's bloom,
And earth in winding sheets of snow lay dressed:
When lo! beside our lattice, seeking rest,
We saw a wild dove smooth her storm-tossed plume:
Her soft eye, fearless, ranged our sheltered room,
Nor shrank when wondering childhood near her pressed.
Then were we comforted: our sad hearts knew
In that confiding bird an emblem true
Of trustful weakness, clinging to the strong:
Nay! a yet holier meaning might belong
To our meek guest: we thought on Christ's Great Gift
Sent down from desolate earth man's soul to lift.

    February, 1887.

A Penitent.

COME Sleep, Death's twin, beside my pillow stand,
    For I am weary of the glaring sun
Long hours before his midway course is run :
O give me rest from sorrow : lay thine hand
On my hot brow, with cooling touch and bland :
Bid the dim future, like a veilèd nun,
Stand by until my brief repose is done ;
Then will I rise and follow through the land.
Where will she lead ? Her vanished sister led
Through mirth and folly on to guilt and dread :
Now skies will darken, flowers shed their bloom,
Birds hush their songs, where'er my footsteps roam :
All thou may'st hope, O heart of mine, from hence,
Must be the peace that waits on penitence.

Development.

THE infant, ere the vital breath begin
    To heave his little breast, doth hidden lie
Close shut from sight and sound : God's earth and sky
First ope to him their wondrous treasuries in
That moment when this life of sense and sin
Finds earliest utterance in a feeble cry :
Thence, day by day, the bright, enquiring eye,
Keen ear, quick touch, new strength and knowledge win.
And we believe that when the Spirit wings
From our cold clay her marvellous flight she knows
Changes yet greater than the embryo's ;
For earth's loud noise, the song the seraph sings,
For earth's rude glare, 'light not on sea or land' :
Born through Death's pangs to all her powers demand.

Maternal Joy.

WHY is the mother glad when first she sees
  The light of life shine in her infant's eyes?
If all the schoolmen teach be true, her cries
Should vex the heavens, while upon trembling knees
She would entreat that blessed death might seize
The child she bore, ere yet he risk the prize
Thousands *must* lose, for one who, pure and wise,
And blest by God, from sin and judgment flees.
The mother-heart rebels—it cannot be!
God gave her joy: that, like Himself, is true!
It were not so if, when the trumpet's sound
Awakes the slumberers in earth and sea,
The Christ, all-loving, comes to claim the few,
While Satan, hating, holds his millions bound.

Cathedral Windows.

THRO' the Cathedral vast and dim I strayed
  While chanted vespers hallowed dying day;
By feeble tapers seen, all cold and grey,
The windows loomed beneath the arches' shade:
But when with dawn I came, I saw, arrayed
In Heaven's own hues, those late dark shapes display
Their pictured legends, while each tinted ray
Like some bright bird on roof and pillar played.
On Man I mused, God's temple, even so
Lit from within, its life how dull, how cold!
The soul, fair window, deepest darkness knows:
But let the sun stream thro' it once, and lo!
Transformed it shines with Heaven's own glorious gold,
Which, to the perfect day, more brightly glows.

"Himself He cannot save."

"HIMSELF He cannot save"! O, blest reply,
  Himself He *will* not save! Thou sneering Jew,
Couldst thou the host of radiant angels view
Who watch their dying Lord, lest one slight sigh
Should call their legions from the farthest sky
To succour and destroy—how would'st thou rue,
And with confused face for aye eschew,
In dust and ashes low, thy shameless lie!
Yet greater shame is ours, if, having known
Not only Christ in suffering on the Tree,
But risen in power, exalted to His Throne,
We still refuse in Him our God to see;
Still turn alike from Cross and open Grave,
And with cold hearts declare "He cannot save!"

Easter Eve, 1883.

Flight.

SHOULD one, who has been blind, behold the plume
  Of some wild bird wave, float in air and swerve,
Still painting on the sky's soft blue the curve
Of grace, what mood soever it assume:
Some miracle of force he must presume
Sways the slight wing, thrills through the tender nerve
For ne'er might he by sense of touch observe
Aught thus defiant of the common doom.
But yet no miracle is wrought; and one,
Long time familiar with the frequent sight,
Perceives no marvel in that airy flight.
My soul! The flight thou waitest, strange and lone
To angels is familiar: trust His skill
Who made all law to mould it to His will.

Prophets of Despair.

YE Prophets not of hope, but of despair,
　　Who preach a faith unworthy of the name,
A love none higher than yourselves may claim,
Who fain would stifle every voice of prayer,
Raze to the ground each sanctuary fair,
And bid man live for earth, from whence he came;
Ye are your own high gods, and who shall blame,
If for none other ye vouchsafe to care?
But wait awhile—when cometh presently,
Death with its dread, perchance its agony,
Will ye not feel ye have too dearly bought
Your vaunted monarchy in realms of thought?
Will ye not lift at last weak hands to Heaven?
True to an instinct only God has given.

An Appeal.

I HEAR the calm stern voice of science say
　　That for the generations yet to come
Each man must toil, nor heed his single doom:
That he, at best, but groweth old and grey
To see his kindred pass for aye away:
That, when his race attains life's highest bloom,
It shall, as surely, fill a hopeless tomb,
As its unhappy ancestor, to-day.
O science, cruel science, tell us why
The strongest yearnings human spirits know,
Unlike all others, are a mockery.
Till thou to this appeal an answer show,
We keep our faith and love, and, at the worst,
Trust life for most is blest, for none accurst.

Faith's Trial.

Non Deos vulgi negare profanum ; sed vulgi opiniones Diis applicare profanum.—EPICURUS.

I.

YES! it is even so! fraud, rapine, greed,
   Rage on the earth, and riot in the air ;
From the fierce tiger, crouching in his lair,
To the small lizard, hiding 'neath a weed,
Each thro' his neighbour's pain supplies his need,
And each must still of treachery beware,
Suspecting when most blest a hidden snare.
That evil rules seems Nature's desperate creed.
Yea, even the swallow as she glances by,
The seeming type of leisure frolicking,
Doth in one flight a myriad lives destroy :
While, a dread shadow o'er her cruel joy,
The watchful hawk with scaly claw, floats high,
Ready to strike the life from her swift wing.

II.

Now turn and watch a bird above her young
Stoop her tired wing to fill their eager throats,
And listen to the loud triumphant notes
From yon near branches by her fond mate sung :
How merrily each joyful change is rung !
" Love and delight ! delight and love " ! it floats
On spring's sweet air, misty with happy motes,
While glad lambs skip the grassy meads among.
And, O remember, weary pessimist,
These joys return with spring's returning days,
Oft-times to many, who may only know
Death once, a swift and unexpected blow.
For these life's pleasure far its pain outweighs,
For these, at least, 'tis blessed to exist.

III.

But say for man, for proud and lonely man,
Born, if to higher joys, to fiercer pains,
With eyes that search the heavens, while he remains
A prisoner in a narrow fixed span,
Bounded by birth and death : is God's great plan
Complete for him, whose life too oft contains
No thrill of joy, small love, less hope, but stains
Of sin, his birthright since his race began ?
We talk of Heaven, of joy beyond the grave,
A Saviour's love, but how avail they him
Born in far distant ages strange and dim,
Or, born to day where all things round deprave ?
Can truths he has not known, or may not know,
Annul his past, or heal his present woe ?

IV.

Hear science speak : in no uncertain tone—
Man's race improves, she says each æon past
Leaves him a nobler being than the last
Saw at its close—though for himself alone,
With those he prizeth most, his loved, his own,
He to the careless winds all hope may cast—
Still for the *race* there opes a prospect vast
Of happiness and peace as yet unknown.
But still we sigh, and ask, "Can this console,
This far dim hope, for all the groans and cries
That have arisen, and even now arise ?"
A cruel mockery seems that promised goal,
As if the breeze of some new wakened spring
Should stir the feathers of a broken wing.

V.

May we not hope that there is hope for all ?
For never can the loving heart receive
That which stern schoolmen tell us they believe,
That some are born to rise, and some to fall :
If God be good—if that we justice call
Is His—may not the future hour retrieve
The painful past, till none at last shall grieve,
Till life's full cup shall hold no drop of gall ?
At last! at last! O Christ who once didst preach
To prisoned souls, it may be, even now,
Within their vast mysterious Hades, Thou
Dost once again a glorious Gospel teach :
That Thou art love, whate'er man's joy or grief,
" Lord we believe, help thou our unbelief " !

Folded Wings.

ONE summer eve I marked a lonely gull
    Stand on a rock, in a tempestuous place ;
The white waves hissing tossed as to embrace
The fearless bird; but, tho' the scene was full
Of wild weird beauty, nothing in his dull
Plain aspect pleased : across the rock's dark face
I watched him creep, no slightest hint of grace
In motion or in form might fancy cull.
But suddenly two silvery pinions wide
From his high shoulders sprang ; he rose, and then
Upon the sunset sky, slow darkening,
Painted that curve which nature's magic pen
Repeateth still unwearied :—soft I sighed,
" O earth, thou chainest many a glorious wing !

To some Modern Poets.

O POETS! Poets!, I marvel ye can sing
    Still in sweet numbers from a hopeless heart
That hath for evermore forsworn its part
In Him who is this fair creation's King:
Since dead for you truths spiritual, which fling
Light upon nature's truths, your highest art
Has lost—how much?—and sunk, at one fell dart,
From an immortal to a mortal thing.
Yet oh! so strong the spell of poesy,
Ye must sing on, even while ye sadly hold
That, when death's kiss shall leave your pale lips cold,
No Power may wake again their melody:
O that some seraph bright to earth might wing
His way, to point you to all music's spring!

POEMS.

Seagulls

ABOVE THE DUBLIN QUAYS.

WHY come ye here? birds of the silver wing,
  Oh rash adventurers who dare to bring
 Such stainless purity of breast and plume
Up the swift stream, that dark and darker grew
The farther that ye left the ocean blue,
 The nearer that ye reached the city's gloom.

For you, in vain, your restless comrades call
With that shrill cry, perchance unmusical,
 Yet with a nameless beauty of its own,
Born of its union with unfettered grace,
And the wild freedom of the lonely place
 Where, of all living sounds, it speaks alone.

Have ye forgotten those untrodden caves,
In whose dim solitudes the winds and waves
 Preserve for ever your unquestioned reign?
Have ye forgotten, 'midst the crowd and noise
Of the loud city, all your ocean joys?
 Oh why, remembering, turn ye not again?

Thus questioned busy Fancy as I stood,
And o'er the Liffey's dark and sullen flood
   Watched the white-wingèd wanderers come and go,
Untroubled by the turmoil of the street,
The whirl of wheels, the tramp of hurrying feet,
   With languid grace still wheeling to and fro.

Then spoke birds in Fancy's mystic tone,
Unto the spirit audible alone,
   Replying "Know our hidden path and fate
As clearly traced before the Omniscient lie
As those of stars that fill His midnight sky,
   Or angel-hosts who on His bidding wait.

"Whither He guided, thither are we come,
The Hand that led us from our ocean home
   Will lead us safely back, but ere we flee
Again to haunts familiar, and to rest
Within the great cliff's broad and sheltering breast,
   Awhile we share thy shade its light to be.

"For thou mayst see in every snowy plume
That glides unscathed above the river's gloom,
   How, o'er the troubled tide of toil and strife,
May stainless move the pure and holy soul,
Within the world, yet free from its control,
   Bearing above the waves a charmèd life.

"And even here, within the busy mart,
A brighter vision yet may reach thine heart,
   And our winged forms to thee be emblems fair
Of those angelic ones who float unseen
O'er weary sufferers in life's struggle keen,
   Their griefs to soothe, their burdens sad to share.

"And yet once more, our beauty and our grace
May haply bear thee, for a little space,
   Far from these narrow scenes of want and care,
Bidding thy soul upon our feathers free
Fly hence to learn, beside the glorious sea,
   That Love yet lives, that Nature still is fair."

Sank the sweet voice—the quiet evening hour
Drew slowly on, and with its gentle power
   Dispersed the crowd, and bid the tumult cease.
The shadows fell, back to their sheltering bay
The graceful sea-birds took their homeward way,
   And the last whisper Fancy breathed was "Peace!"

Bereavement.

And can we smile when thou art dead?
  Aye, Brother, even so,
The rose of summer will be red,
  In spite of winter's snow.
                    O. W. HOLMES.

STRANGE is it, even in this sad world of ours,
   So full of darkness and of mystery,
That each man's life, for him endowed with powers
   To gain, or lose, a blest eternity,

Must pass away, and, life surrounding seem
   A course unmoved to hold, as, dim and vain,
Even as the fancies of a faded dream,
   Were his past share in both its joy and pain.

The bird will carol to the closèd ear,
    The sun will shine upon the darkened eye,
And, all unconscious of the shrouded bier,
    Nature preserve her wonted harmony.

Even fellow-men whose steps with theirs bygone
    Have often crossed in toil or pleasûre's way,
But lightly heed, when death's dark shadow thrown
    Athwart it, turns to night another's day.

Yes, and even they whose tender hearts could boast
    The sweetest converse with the spirit fled,
Who lonely weep above their prized and lost
    Such tears as only love bereaved may shed,

Though hope seem buried in the new-made grave,
    Must feel, as Time's unresting tide rolls on,
Sad memories, washed by its Lethean wave,
    Fade, and still fade, till they well-nigh are gone.

Till, strangest mood of any human mind,
    A vague regret will come for sorrow flown,
And the weak heart, blaming itself, shall find
    That Time's swift stream too well its work hath done.

O fond weak heart! that cannot, will not, see
    The loving rule the hurrying tide obeys,
That fain would dwell in lonely misery
    Amidst dim after-glows of vanished days.

O fond weak heart! unthinking, and unwise,
    That heeds nor want nor sorrow save its own,
That fain would find all nature's sympathies,
    Glad or regretful, with itself alone.

Is it not better far that Nature should
   Rule as she will her universal realm,
Than glooming, gladdening, with thy changeful mood,
   Bid joy enervate, sorrow overwhelm?

Is it not better far that Time should still
   The first wild throbs of anguish and despair,
Than leave thee, victim of a rebel will,
   To make a selfish grief thine only care?

How wilt thou battle with the ills of life
   If all thy strength lie buried in the grave?
How bear thee boldly in the constant strife
Of truth with falsehood, if to grief a slave?

Let it console thee, this effacing Time,
   Even while it dimmeth, halloweth the past,
Till, but with holy aims and hopes sublime,
   Is linked the memory of our dead at last.

Then mourn thou not if as Time rolleth on
   Some treasured memories slowly vanish here,
Though the sad solace that they gave be gone,
   Heaven guards them all!—we shall remember there!

   Advent Sunday, 1870.

The Sparrow's Flight.

A GROUP of warriors in their banquet hall,
   Around their monarch gathered, draughts of mead
From carven cups in deep libations quaff;
And loud and long of battle-fields they sing,
Of heroes old, of arms invincible,
Of daring deeds, of demons driven to death.

Quiet and calm amidst the clamorous crew
One warrior sits, broad-browed and earnest-eyed;
He recks not of the revelry, but whets
His ponderous sword against to-morrow's fight.
For him life has no holiday; he holds
That sharp sword dearer than a thousand songs.

There comes a pause in the rude revelry,
And in that pause the thoughtful warrior hears
Against the roof a rush of restless wings:
From his stern work he lifts his eyes, and when,
Amidst the rough-hewn rafters of the place,
They rest upon a little frightened bird,
Their fierce light softens, and the gazer seems
As by some sudden sorrow overcome:
Unheeded on the floor his weapon rings,
And deeply musing for short space he sits,
Then to the King he turns, and these his words
Make a long silence in the noisy hall.

" To me it seems, O King, when we compare
This present life with those dark days that were
Ere it began, and which return again,
Its brief space past—to me it seems as when—
Whiles thou art sitting as thou sittest now,
The storm without, within the fire's bright glow,—
Lured by the rays that thro' the loopholes rise,
In at the open door a sparrow flies,
Flutters a moment restlessly, and then
Back to the gloom it fled returns again,
Out thro' another door. This have I seen
But now, O mighty King, and it has been
To me a sign with saddest meaning rife
Of the dark mystery of this our life.
What time the trembling bird was here 'twas free
Alike from tempest and from gloom; yet see

How scant the peaceful interval! anon
From storm to storm it passed, and it was gone :
Nor might who marked its rapid passage know
Whence it had come, or whither it would go.
Lo! thus our life! one moment it is seen,
The next, is fled, as it had never been.
What lies beyond the gates of birth and death
No poet singeth, and no seer saith,
And ah! most bitter in our cup of woe
Is the sad knowledge that we may not know."

1867.

Love's Decision.

"BRING the prisoner"! cries the monarch :
    Royal minions lead him out,
While the crowd around the palace
    Greet him with malignant shout.

Do the people love their monarch,
    Grieving with a loyal soul
That a comrade all unworthy
    Spurns his firm and wise control?

Nay, not so, but trodden under
    By a despot's iron will,
They the self-preserving instincts
    Of low natures thus fulfil.

Not of them the noble captive,
    Moving slow, with step of pride,
Though with fettered wrists and ankles,
    And stern guards on either side.

He has dared to feel desire
    For a fair forbidden thing;
He has dared, bold man, to aspire
    To the daughter of his King.

Now he treads the court of trial,
    And before the monarch stands,
And men look that he should falter,
    With bent knees, and clasped hands.

But he bears himself as proudly
    As young palm-tree straight and tall,
Seeking one fair presence only
    In the crowded judgment-hall.

Cries the monarch in his anger,
    "Does the base-born villain dream
That the blood of hinds and peasants
    Shall pollute the royal stream?

"Through a line of kings it reached me,
    And must pass untainted on:
Never shall a subject's offspring
    Fill my sire's ancestral throne.

"Yet, I own the youth hath spirit,
    And a face both proud and fair,
And he neither pales nor trembles
    Here before my judgment chair.

"Know I how to test his courage!
    See, on either side the throne
Closèd iron doors—between them
    He must choose—and enter one.

" Each a different fate concealeth,
   Choose he ill—a tiger's claws
Tear the heart from out his bosom
   Who has dared defy my laws.

" Choose he well—a lovely maiden
   Greets him, herald fair of life,
And I rule that he shall take her,
   Ere the sunset hour to wife."

Mark the princess where she standeth
   Silent near her father's throne,
Pale and trembling as a lily
   By a sudden tempest blown.

She has learned the secret hidden
   By each sealed iron gate,
And she knows her power to rescue
   Or consign to cruel fate.

Will she save her reckless lover?
   Will she doom to death forlorn?
Do those drooping eyelids cover
   Love, indifference, or scorn?

Lo! beneath her gentle bosom
   Furious conflict rages now,
All the fiercer for the quiet
   Throned upon her lip and brow.

At her face her lover glances:
   Shall her glance refuse to save
From the tiger's rude embraces
   And a low dishonoured grave?

Or, shall she with heart unflinching,
  Bid him clasp an unsought bride,
And through all the dreary future
  Watch her happy at his side?

Or, a calm indifference feigning,
  Give no sign, and take no heed—
While she holds the cruel balance
  Fast the fatal moments speed.

Either way her fond heart breaketh,
  Either way her fair hopes die,
But at least she may deliver
  From a death of agony.

Once again the roses hover
  O'er her lovely brow, the while
Swift she glances at her lover,
  Saves—resigns him—with a smile.

'Tis her last! faint, cold, and breathless,
  Sinks she at her father's feet
In the arms of death, sole bridegroom
  For a maid so hapless meet.

A Lament.

PRELUDE.

AH me! ah me! the song I sing
  As old, yet fresh, as earth and sky,
On many a fond heart's tenderest string
Has lived and died, now nerved to fling
  The passion of its music high,
Now faltering as the wounded wing
  That bears the dove apart to die.

Yet, but for those who never knew
    How closely pleasure clings to pain,
Who scarcely hold that singer true
Who, seeking solace, doth imbue
    With his heart's grief his sweetest strain—
Only for those—the heartless few—
    The oft-told tale is told in vain.

Most, taught by sad experience, know
    To speak its sorrow soothes the mind
That sees its tree of promise low,
Fair budding flowers that might not blow,
    All scattered to the unpitying wind,
The sunny spring-tide's glorious show
    That might no ripening summer find.

SONG.

Ah Love! fair tyrant o'er the young,
    Why did thy gilded fetters fall
About my neck?—so lightly flung,
    Thy captive scarcely felt the thrall.

I loved, and that I was beloved,
    Too vain, too innocent, believed.
False has my lover's promise proved,
    O cruelly has he deceived!

For surely if, beneath God's sky,
    Fair seeming troth was ever given,
'Twas when he swore the fatal lie
    That gave my life a glimpse of heaven.

A glimpse that left that life to be
   More dark, more lonely, than before—
A bark that shunned the open sea,
   But to be wrecked upon the shore.

And is he happy? who may tell?
   Perchance he breathes in other ears
The flattering tale he practised well
   Between my answering smiles and tears.

But yet I will not curse him; no!
   I would not break his careless rest,
Nor wake one pang of selfish woe
   Within that cold unfeeling breast.

For my ill-fated love, ah me!
   With mingled pride and shame, I own,
Still clings, like ivy, to the tree,
   Whence all that wooed her clasp is gone.

London,

1887-8.

I.

WINTER on stormy wings
   Forth from his stronghold springs,
And his keen arrows flings
   Thro' the wide air:
Childhood's bright smiles are quenched,
Tears women's cheeks have drenched,
Men stand, their fierce teeth clenched,
   Dumb with despair.

II.

See Winter's hell-hounds bold,
Hunger, disease, and cold,
With all their brood untold,
    Waiting their prey:
Vainly would man's weak hand,
Clutching a rope of sand,
With many a broken strand,
    Keep them at bay.

III.

O Thou, the Good and Great,
Ere it be all too late,
Look from Thine high estate
    On earth below:
Hear how Thy foes proclaim,
With lips that know not shame,
That Thou art but a name,
    Mocking our woe.

IV.

Thou, who when famine's night
Threatened Thine Israel's flight,
*Mad'st earth with manna white,
    Heaven black with quails,
Are all Thy prophets dumb?
May no strong rescue come
From Love's eternal home,
    When nature fails?

---

* The Writer is indebted for the idea contained in this and the following line to an eloquent Sermon heard in Leeds Parish Church, July, 1888.

V.

In this our later day
Wilt Thou no might display
Howe'er Thy people pray
    With tear and moan?
While unbelievers sneer,
" Cry ye, but none can hear,
He whom ye love and fear
    Is as a stone.

VI.

" Deem ye He hath forgot?
Nay He existeth not,
Blind chance directs your lot,
    Blind chance or fate:
Kneel on the barren ground,
Call till the hills resound,
Yet is no answer found,
    Unchanged your state.

VII.

" Built upon fables old,
Evermore told, re-told,
Is the false faith ye hold:
    Now, reason's light,
Shining with purer ray,
Doth on these visions play;
Like mist they melt away
    From the cleared sight."

  ·   ·   ·   ·   ·   ·

VIII.

Shall we who love Thee, Lord,
We who still trust Thy Word,
Who in our hearts have heard
    Speech from above:
We who have yearnings high
For perfect purity
Earth cannot satisfy;
    Instincts of love,

IX.

Humble and holy fear,
Towards One we must revere,
Never demanded here
    By aught around:
Instincts of glorious hope,
Passing the narrow scope
Of joys on earth that grope,
    By the grave bound.

X.

Shall we give up our faith,
    Whate'er the Tempter saith,
Doubt, the pale ghost of Death,
    Science, or Scorn?
No! though we feel the night,
Yet will we look for light,
Waiting at last the bright
    Breaking of morn.

XI.

    Conscious that finite man
    May not presume to scan
    That vast eternal plan
        Which God hath wrought:
    Trusting that in the end
    All will be seen to tend
    Towards bliss that shall transcend
        Man's highest thought!

"Ye Faerie Rose."

HOW oft will memories of its childhood cling
    About the life mature, and with them bring
Such keen emotion both to heart and brain,
That 'neath grey hairs young pulses throb again.

I do remember in the days when youth
Was strong in innocent belief in truth,
I saw a flower which to my dazzled eyes
Seemed meet to bloom in bowers of Paradise,

Yclept "Y^e Faerie Rose," and with that word
What vague delight my childish bosom stirred!
That rose had been, whate'er the wise repeat,
By any other name *less* fair and sweet.

Each dainty blossom of the small tree stood
Full-blown, yet tinier than another's bud,
It might have nodded on an elf-king's crest,
Or shed its fragrance from a fay's soft breast.

And one, who saw the longing well betrayed
By my too eager gaze, kind promise made
That I, ere long, should for mine own possess
What seemed a very fount of happiness.

That fairy flower, while childish trust was strong,
Made bright my days, and shone my dreams among,
But months swept by, and still the hope that thrilled
Each fibre of my heart was unfulfilled.

And even now, when memory of the pain
That disappointment gave me wakes again,
In spite of deeper griefs of added years,
'Tis fain to fill these faded eyes with tears.

Oh! ye, who hold within your loving grasp
A young child's trust, see to it that ye clasp
With tender touch the frailest flower that blows,
Snap not from its slight stem life's "faerie rose."

The Unknown Future.

SHE comes, the dreadful form, with veilèd brow,
    Finger on lip, and eyes that downward turn;
She tramples thro' my garden, treading low
Its springing buds, and quenching all the glow
    Where its late roses burn.

To her is sacred neither time nor place;
    She comes and peers into my secret bowers,
Uplifts her veil a moment, and her face
Casts a dark shadow on the hallowed space,
    As o'er its bliss she glowers.

She stoops, and whispers in my spirit's ear,
    "How long? Thou hast been happy! All have woe!
What right hast thou earth's blessedness to share,
And not partake that heritage of care
    Which all her children know?"

I make reply, "Grief has been mine, my heart
    Was sorely riven when blossoms twain were torn
From its strong tendrils by stern Death apart:
I have known grief—aye, and its keenest smart,
    Past is life's summer morn."

Then she retorteth, "Fool! and dost thou deem
    That thou for evermore art quits with grief?
Dost thou not own—tho' the confession seem
An insult to thy dead—they do not dream
    Who say, 'Time brings relief?'"

"Know, full many a wingèd shaft and naked spear
    Lie waiting in my silent armoury,
Whose speed and flash shall startle eye and ear,
And thrill thy spirit with a nameless fear,
    Even when they pass thee by.

"But some! they shall strike home! I say not when,
    I dare not say how many or how few,
Perchance their name is 'Legion'—in my ken
I hold them all—and the approaching 'then'
    Shall prove my knowledge true.

"Amidst my weapons well thou know'st that one
    Must blanch thy cheek, must stay thy quivering breath;
That thou, by friends surrounded—yet alone—
Must wait the dart inevitable, thrown
    By the sure hand of Death.

"Prepare thee! O prepare thee! Even now
  Set all thine house in order: turn thy face
Unto the wall: bend thy proud spirit low:
While tears of penitential sorrow flow,
    The guilty past retrace.

"Then He who guides my footsteps, holds my hand,
  Who sent me hither to commune with thee,
And utter my dark speech, at last may stand
Beside thee—and, for my pale form, a band
    Of angels thou may'st see.

"And then, perchance, they too shall prophesy,
  But, joys beyond thy best imaginings,
Shall show thee, safe in Heaven's high treasury,
Thy vanished loves, shall bear thy spirit free
From sorrow, pain, and sin's dark mystery,
    Hence on their outspread wings."

Lent, 1887.

In Memoriam.

SIR E. LANDSEER, R.A., OB. 1873.

LANDSEER, farewell! reluctantly we write
  On England's death-roll now thine honoured name,
Which needs no record to preserve it bright,
  For, long as Art survives, lives Landseer's fame.

England will mourn thee, sadly will retrace
  Thy past, and all its golden days review,
Recall the well-known form, the kindly face,
  Dear to the many, dearer to the few.

And then, love's tribute paid, will slowly turn
  To mark the work those skilful fingers wrought,
And reverently from the great Master learn
  Whate'er of good and truth his pencil taught.

Perchance some shallow cynic turns to ask,
  " Why raise this man above his fellow men ?
For the great world he hath performed no task
  Save what may charm some idler now and then."

Well ! be it so ! is Beauty nothing worth ?
  Is Pleasure nothing in this world of pain ?
Why smile the flowers ? why ring the groves with mirth ?
  Is the bloom idle ? is the music vain ?

But Landseer has done more—his pencil pleads
  For the brute race with our humanity—
His skilful hand has pictured faithful deeds,
  Which claim and win our love and sympathy.

O who, with spirit all unmoved can mark
  The Collie sitting by the bier alone,
The only mourner in that chamber dark,
  Whence human friendship, human love are gone ?

Or see, while leaps the breaker white with foam,
  The brave Newfoundland dare its angry crest,
To snatch the tender babe, and bear it home
  From that wild pillow to its mother's breast ?

Look where beneath the door a creeping stream
  Wakes in the waiting hound no idle fears ;
What fond affections in the fixed eyes gleam !
  How the true heart seems listening in the ears !

Still, as we muse, familiar pictures rise,
  "The Stag at Bay," "The Monarch of the Glen,"
The canine synod, with its leader wise,
  Aping the manners and the mien of men.

But not alone of love, faith, dignity,
  In the brute race did Landseer's pencil teach :
Look, where the hunted stag, all wearily,
  Gains at the sunset-hour the island-beach.

Surely the artist pondered, as his hand
  With gentlest touches limned that tender sky,
On that dark hour, when, parted from the band
  Of workers, he must lay him down and die.

Surely, the holier musings of his mind
  Are uttered in that scene, so soft and fair,
And the sweet fancy, by his art enshrined,
  Is less a picture than a silent prayer.

We, with that thought will trust him to the grave,
  Where sleeping midst the great and good he lies ;
And every lesson that his pencil gave,
  Even as the trophies of his art will prize.

Love's Seasons.

TOGETHER we wandered, my Playmate and I,
  When the earth was an emerald, a sapphire the sky,
When each breath of the breeze brought new beauties to birth,
And the soaring lark seemed the freed spirit of mirth ;

When the primrose and windflower starr'd coppice and brae,
And the woodlands were white with the snows of the May:
Then we tasted youth's joy, but the bright, bubbling flow
Of its spring scarcely told where its waters would go.

Together we wandered, my Lover and I,
When the full blaze of summer shone down from the sky,
When its murmurous music lulled life to repose,
And the butterfly dreamed on the breast of the rose;
When the turtle-dove cooed to her mate in the bowers,
And the earth was a cushion of moss and of flowers:
Then we quaffed Love's sweet draught—the light waters danced so,
That they caught every colour of phantasy's bow.

Together we wandered, my Husband and I,
When the light fell, down ladders of mist, from the sky,
When the air was so still that we heard, as we stood,
The ripe chestnut drop in the many-hued wood,
On its carpet of gold, while the swallow, coy guest
Of the sunshine, glanced by on her wings of unrest:
Then content brimmed our cup, for Love's fount of delight
Had o'erflowed its fair banks in a stream broad and bright.

Together we wandered, my old Man and I,
When hardly one ray pierced the storm-laden sky,
Yet the robin, 'midst berries as red as his breast,
Piped on, while the snow filled his desolate nest;
And we knew, tho' it seemed to be shrouding decay,
It was sheltering the buds of another fair May:
Then sweet hope cheered our hearts, for Love's stream had become
A calm river that swept to its infinite Home.

A Birch Tree

IN GLYNSOUTHWELL, CO. DUBLIN.

LOOK on October's woods, and say
  If the soft lustre of decay
May not compare with robes of May.

This eve I marked a fairy band
Of Autumn-tinted birches stand,
Flanked by dark pines on either hand.

But one apart and lonely stood,
Upon the confines of the wood,
Lovelier than all the sisterhood.

While those, in evening's mellow light,
Showed like princesses, tall and slight,
In robes of festal gold bedight.

This, all in airy lightness drest,
Shone out against the grove's dark breast,
As if the wanton Sun, in jest,

Thrusting from heaven a magic lance,
Had touched a fountain in its dance,
And held it in a breathless trance.

One almost watched for golden spray
Upon the earth to fall and play,
Then, in bright ripples, roll away.

Ne'er did the Spring, with all its sheen,
Of quivering light, thro' arches green,
Delight me with a fairer scene.

And oh! if autumn woods can show
A radiance that no Spring may know,
I will not mourn my youth, altho'

Life's Winter comes to bare my trees,
To chill me with its icy breeze,
And every fount of joy to freeze.

Who knows but some entrancing glow
May shine across its drifted snow,
Ere 'neath earth's tender shroud I go?

Oh! long in memory's treasury,
A wand of that enchanted tree
Shall wear its golden bloom for me!

The Birch Tree in Winter.

MY fountain shed at last its spray,
    Falling in glittering dust away,
And left a slender spectre gray,

Which, bending to each breeze that blew,
Still kept a shadowy beauty through
The wildest storms December knew,

While sturdier trees all warped and torn,
O'er scattered branches stood forlorn—
Sport of the wind that laughed in scorn.

And yet I passed unnoticed by
My tree—or only looked, to sigh
Over a golden memory.

Heedless I deemed its glory gone,
Or waited its return alone,
When winter's dreary months were flown.

I little thought that shadowy tree
Another lesson kept for me
For darker hours, till, suddenly,

As one dull morning slowly broke,
The Snow-King of the North awoke,
And touched, as with a magic stroke,

The spectre grey, and in its place,
All veiled in snow mine eyes could trace
Again my tree of fount-like grace.

Again, supremely fair it stood
Above its sisters of the wood,
Lending itself to every mood

Of the swift year's caprice—and still,
In winter, as in autumn chill,
Showed lovelier for each touch of ill.

Nor strength nor fury might deform
The tree that bowed before the storm,
And kept unchanged its springtide form;

For beauty's outline lay beneath
The curves of every snowy wreath,
With gentle force defying death.

And bright as in October's dream,
The slender branches wore a gleam
That scarcely of the earth might seem:

They shone with such celestial glow,
They whispered of the robes of snow,
Whose stainless glory those shall know,

Who, bending to God's discipline,
Still keep the soul's unsullied shrine
A temple fair for Grace Divine.

In Memoriam.

G. W. F. REICHEL.

St. Mark's Day, 1875.*

AGAIN the sunny April hours
    A blessed Saint recall,
For yet once more on Time's swift wing
    Returns his festival.

But not as when its vernal sun
    Last shone upon our way,
Do we with joyful step and heart
    Keep the glad feast to-day.

Then the white-robed procession moved
    Past many a flowery wreath;
Now, muffled bell and sable fold
    Speak mournfully of death.

One hand that culled our festal flowers
    May no fresh tribute bring;
One eye that watched them fade and pass
    Sees no new blossoms spring.

One heart whose pulse beat high with ours
    Lies calm as summer wave;
One voice that thro' our anthem thrilled
    Is silent in the grave.

No more for us to bear alone
    The thread of melody,
And thro' the maze of music lead
    Its linkèd harmony.

---

* The Dedication Festival of the Chapel of St. Columba's College.

O little life! a spring-tide bud
   Just bursting into bloom,
What promise fair of strength and grace
   Lies blighted in the tomb!

O little life! a quivering harp,
   With half its songs unsung,
How many a chord of joy and pain
   Has death's stern hand unstrung!

Young steps that often carelessly
   Have passed the churchyard ground,
Pausing beside thy grave to-day,
   Will stay their joyous bound.

Yet they who oft with thee have met
   For words and thoughts of Heaven,
And by thy side in fervent prayer
   Before God's throne have striven,

May turn from thoughts of pain and loss
   To gaze upon the sky,
Where He whose arm hath conquered death
   Reigneth in majesty.

And Spring, 'midst haunts thou lovedst well,
   Waking with glowing breath
The glories that have slept awhile
   'Neath winter's rule of death,

Shall whisper to our sorrowing hearts
   Her lesson, often told,
Yet ever sweet and ever new,
   Till faith and love grow cold.

We will not mourn as those whose eyes
   No light thro' darkness see,
But trust, altho' with swelling tears,
   That "it is well" with thee.

Unconscious Happiness.

PURE happiness is an unconscious thing:
　　Such is the lark's, upon his quivering wing;
Nought doth he reck of distance or of speed,
To powers of flight and song he gives no heed,
But towards the zenith is content to soar,
And down the rapture of his spirit pour.

Such the child's happiness; he does not ask
Its whence or why, till joy becomes a task;
He does not analyse the cup he quaffs,
And, when a babe looks in his face, and laughs
For very merriment, he too will smile,
Nor ponder on their mutual mirth the while.

When we begin to question, then we fear,
We sigh, "Too bright to last!"—see, in our clear
Thin atmosphere, the outline of a hill,
By mists long hidden, all unmounted still:
The efflorescence of life's joy is gone,
Nor on this side the grave may be re-won.

"Once, over all."

ONCE, over all, Love's glamour glows,
　　And they are poets then;
Beneath its radiance Nature shows
　　Her face unveiled to men
Who never marked before the coy
　　Shy beauty that she wears,
Nor knew her fellowship in joy,
　　Her sympathy with tears.

They wake, and with a glad surprise,
  To see a thousand things ;
To read the tender prophecies
  The dawn or sunset brings ;
To find the fragrance of the flowers,
  The music of the grove,
All secrets of earth's hidden bowers,
  Interpreted by Love.

Insects there are whose being frail
  Begins in lowly guise ;
Thro' weeds and clay their forms they trail,
  Nor seek from earth to rise,
Till suddenly desire upsprings
  To wanton in the air,
To woo, to mate, and filmy wings
  Their tiny bodies bear.

They mount the ether blue, and know
  A new and strange delight ;
They bathe them in the sunny glow ;
  They feel the joy of flight :
So, when Love comes, life finds its plumes,
  And soars thro' pleasure's sky ;
But ah ! Time also wings assumes,
  And fast he fleeteth by.

Oh ! hours twice winged, with brimming eyes
  We dream you o'er again,
Ye made the earth a Paradise—
  Parting its only pain !
But to have soared your little space
  Thro' Love's sweet light and shade,
Has left with life a tender grace
  That may not wholly fade.

And, when we mark Love rise and shine,
    Within our children's eyes,
We feel again its power divine,
    And fondly sympathise ;
While, watching tenderly, we wait
    To see its fulness shed,
As if, close-linked with others' fate,
    Our own young wooing sped.

For us it gleams an afterglow ;
    For them is dawn begun ;
For us the light is sinking low ;
    For them a rising sun
Is waking with its glorious ray
    The melodies of morn,
And in fair regions far away
    Another day is born.

We hear the song that has been sung
    A thousand, thousand times,
That down the centuries is rung
    Upon eternal chimes :
But till bright eyes shall cease to shine,
    Till youthful hearts grow cold,
Till life the soul of life resign
    It never can be old !

The Ascent of Mount Hor.

NUMBERS XX. 25-28.

BEHOLD them climb the Mount of Hor,
　　That patriarchal pair,
Bound by strong ties of brotherhood,
　　Each other's grief they share :
Together they have fought for God,
　　Together have prevailed,
And, overborne by sin's fierce strife,
　　Together they have failed.

In all his priestly vesture clad,
　　See holy Aaron come,
Led by a Will he must obey,
　　He leaves his tented home,
And, while his hallowed garments sweep
　　The dewy mountain-sod,
He treads the vast and lonely grave
　　For him ordained of God.

But he, the younger man, who moves
　　Slow at his elders' side,
Does he perceive what glory fills
　　That mountain temple wide ?
Or know that in God's Presence there,
　　Robed by his Prophet's hand,
He, as High-Priest of Israel,
　　Shall consecrated stand ?

Perchance, as on Moriah's Mount,
    In distant days of yore,
Not all who climb the toilsome steep
    See Heaven's open door:
Not all—but one, alas too well,
    Doth sadly comprehend
How from its threshold, desolate,
    He must to Earth descend.

Miriam he mourns, whose loving eyes
    Watched o'er his bulrush nest,
Whose guileless art restored the babe
    To its own mother's breast,
Who, filled with true poetic fire,
    Led Israel's minstrel band,
And sang the glory and the bliss
    Of Canaan's promised land.

The hands that tossed the timbrels lie
    Folded in calm repose,
Above the quiet breast, which now
    No pulse of rapture knows:
For she, whose psalm the Red Sea waves
    While yet they roll, prolong,
Has crossed a fiercer tide, to sing
    A grander triumph song.

Aaron in other days upheld
    His brother's failing powers,
When Israel strove with Amalek
    Thro' long and weary hours:
Now must the younger brother watch
    The elder's sinking breath,
And feel the hands that strengthened his
    Cold in the clasp of death.

What marvel if sad longings fill
  The aged patriarch's breast,
To share, as he their toil hath shared,
  His brethren's quiet rest:
Perchance on his prophetic gaze
  There looms another hill,
Where he, alone with God and Death,
  Must suffer and be still.

O mystery of Providence!
  That, of the chosen three,
Whose faith and love led Israel forth,
  O'er desert sand, and sea,
Not one might reach that lovely land,
  The home of his desire,
But each, with heart unsatisfied,
  Must in the wild expire.

But ah! who knows what glorious blaze
  Of unimagined light,
As Earth grew dark, from Heaven fell
  Upon their dying sight,
Revealing not fair Canaan's fields,
  Where milk and honey flowed,
But lighting all the stream of life
  Around the Throne of God!

To the South Wind.

FLY forth, sweet breeze, on happy task to roam,
    Fly from the burning bosom of the sun,
Nor sleep again within thy tropic home
    Till all thy work of gladness shall be done.

Fly forth! fly forth! in woodlands brown and sere
    Blow wide green leaves, and bare the lily's breast;
To all that droopeth, whisper, "Spring is here"!
    And, lingering on the violet bank to rest,

Kiss every bud to bloom—in vale, on hill,
    Bid winter's footprints vanish at thy breath,
While, ere they fall, revivèd earth to chill,
    The snowflakes flutter in thine arms to death.

Aid the fond labours of the brooding dove,
    Waving thy fostering pinions o'er her own,
Still lingering near her little world of love
    Till all its tender cares be fledged and flown.

Fly to the city, pierce its smoky pall,
    Wave in the murky air thy perfumed wings,
Till many a worn and wearied heart recall
    In fragrant memories its faded springs.

Go, greet the Child, meet playmate for the young,
    The pulses of his spirit dance with thee.
Be his brief lesson by thy soft lips sung
    A sweet south wind amidst life's storms to be.

Go to the agèd man, and whisper low,
  As o'er his hoary brow he feels thee play,
Of heavenly gales ere long for him to blow,
  Where life, for ever young, knows no decay.

Creep to the sick man's chamber, even there,
  Where Death seems lord, prove mightier influence rife,
And softly murmur in the dying ear,
  "I am the Resurrection and the Life."

And stay not yet: even to the churchyard bring
  Thy soothing presence, and all silently,
Above the flowering turf this anthem sing,
  "Where, Death, thy sting? Where, Grave, thy victory?"

Faded Heather.

RELIC of the summer,
  One small heather spray.
From my frost-bound windows
  Tempts mine eyes away
And I fix them idly
  On its dusky bloom,
Till past scenes of beauty
  Fill my narrow room.

Soft hills rise before me,
  By fleet sunbeams kissed,
Now in distance fading,
  Now in fleecy mist.

Here a bold crag showeth
    Clear against the sky;
There a dimple darkens
    Where a tarn doth lie.

And, while fancy lingers
    O'er those faded bells
Hear I all the music
    Of the upland fells:
Now the slow bee's humming
    O'er ambrosial food,
Now the whirr of startled birds
    Shy from solitude.

Aye, so keen the sense in
    Fancy's atmosphere,
That the sudden snapping
    Of the gorse I hear,
Though above are sounding
    Those wild bugles blown
From his chariot, by the wind,
    Leaving throne for throne.

Shines again the morning
    Of that summer day
When the buds were gathered
    Of my heather spray:
Once again I wander
    Thro' Glen-Cullen Pass,
Tread the velvet softness
    Of its wayside grass.

And a little maiden,
    Lissom, slight and fair,
With her soft eyes shining
    'Neath her golden hair,

Trippeth on before me
　With a step as free
As the dancing wavelet
　Of the summer sea.

Eagerly she searches
　For the brightest bud,
Now of ling, now heather,
　In capricious mood:
Now she climbs a boulder,
　Now she leaps a brook,
Then bears back her treasures
　With triumphant look.

Tenderly she holds them
　In her slender hand,
For, those hill-born blossoms
　By cold breezes fanned,
Must be nursed as fondly
　As exotics rare,
Placed in daintiest china,
　With supremest care.

Long, oh long, my Darling,
　Be thy gentle aim
So to cherish graces
　That from Nature came.
Long may art's vain glamour
　Wear no rival charm,
Fashion with her follies
　Pass thee without harm.

Reared beside the mountain,
　May thy spirit be
Like the breezes blowing
　O'er it from the sea,

Free from noxious vapours,
    Free from feverish heat,
As its brooklets joyous,
    As its blossoms sweet.

Be it still thy mission,
    Wheresoe'er thou rove,
To bear home rich treasure
    Unto hearts that love :
To make bright their winter
    With those summer flowers,
Whose first heavenly radiance
    Lighted Eden's bowers.

Killed by Accident,

September, 18—.

ACROSS the moor, thro' falling mist,
    They bore my Darling home,
His blood the purple heather dyed
    With yet a darker bloom—
That heather, which had well nigh been
    His shroud, and then his tomb.

They laid him in a chamber wide
    Of his own castle fair,
They shut the sunlight out, and then
    They gently led me there,
And in that hour supreme I learned
    What human hearts may bear,

And yet not break—amidst them all
   I stood with him alone,
Love, that had faltered in my heart,
   Climbed an eternal throne :
The dead was all my life, and yet
   I did not cry nor moan—

But felt—ah me ! when comes the hour
   That I shall cease to feel ?
When draws the King of Terrors nigh,
   Not to destroy but heal,
And bid his gentle anodyne
   Over my spirit steal ?

His kindred mourned my love, and shed
   Tears, while I could not weep,
And lavishly sweet flowers they strewed
   Above his place of sleep ;
But now, about his carven name
   Unchecked the mosses creep.

And Nature's teardrops fall alone
   Upon the peaceful sod ;
For months the grass around has sprung,
   By human foot untrod,
And only o'er his quiet rest
   Watches the eye of God.

And now within his boyhood's home
   Another beareth sway,
The hound he loved, the horse he rode,
   A stranger's call obey,
And even his very memory
   Seems passing swift away.

And to my fancy's ear there come
    O'er leagues of heaving sea,
Which now divide the earth that holds
    My one true love from me,
The laugh of mirth, the shout of joy,
    The stir of revelry.

I hear the beat of dancing feet,
    The minstrel harp that tells
Some joyous festival is kept,
    And oh! my heart rebels,
When on the summer breeze is borne
    The clash of marriage bells.

They should have rung for me, and him
    Who sleeps their sound beneath,
While this sweet summer shone—and oh!
    The flowers of that fair wreath,
Which crowneth now the bride's young brow
    Seem garlanded by Death!

Oh heartless bells! but late ye tolled
    Upon the autumnal air,
As if ye had some secret power
    Our mortal griefs to share,
And now, your joyful cadences
    I patiently must bear.

Ah well! nor bliss nor agony
    Again this heart may know,
For I have scaled the heights of joy,
    Sounded the depths of woe,
And only wait—in silence wait—
    Death's footstep, sure but slow.

From the Prose of Shaftesbury.

IMAGINE one, who from an inland home
Unto the coast, till now unseen, is come,
There to behold, in quiet waters moored,
A lonely vessel lie, with none on board.
Behold him, trembling, climb its slippery side,
Scarred by the warfare of the wind and tide,
Then gain the lower deck, and stand to view
The holds for cargo and the berths for crew,
The awning spread, from sun and shower to screen,
The guardian bulwarks, all the varied scene,
He will admire perchance, and understand:
Life has like needs on ocean and on land.

But, if from all below he raise his glance
Up to the summer heaven's serene expanse,
And see dark tracery obstruct his view,
Tall stately masts that lift into the blue
White furlèd sails, and flags, not floating free,
But idly drooping o'er a waveless sea—
How great his wonder! for he may not guess
Their various uses, novelties oppress
Both sight and sense; but, does he thence conclude
That all around his sight and sense delude?
No, rather he surveys with heightened zest
What he may comprehend, and deems the rest
Framed for some purpose strange, beyond his ken,
Yet fraught with blessings for the race of men.

And shall vain man behold, and idly curse,
In his small impotence, the universe,
Because from his too-oft presumptuous gaze
God veils in mystery his higher ways?

Because his puny mind is weak to scan
The mighty scope of an eternal plan?
No! rather let him learn from blessings, spread
Within his vision and beneath his tread,
To trust the Love that rules an empire vast,
And wait the knowledge that will come at last.

Sleep.

BROOD above me, gentle Sleep,
In thy downy chambers deep
Let me sink to happy rest,
There to find what at the best
Waking life may seldom know—
Peace renewed, forgotten woe.

O how often dost thou come
On white wings across the gloom!
Making all the darksome night
Than the brightest day more bright,
Weaving over weary eyes
Subtle webs of phantasies.

In thine arms the poor man gains
Wealth's delights without its pains,
Slumbering 'neath the open sky
Seems on gilded couch to lie,
Ruleth in a palace fair,
King, without palatial care.

Thence, the merchant sees his store
Safely reach, and strew the shore;
Odorous spices, colours rich,
All his slumbering sense bewitch;
Fame and honour on each hand,
Proffering guerdons, seem to stand.

There the lover finds his fair
Gentle as the yielding air,
Gone the haughty glance of scorn
That her lovely brow had worn,
All his pain forgotten is
In the rapture of a kiss.

There the mother clasps again
That sweet babe whom death hath ta'en,
Feels the small lips droop aside,
With love's nectar satisfied:
Brood above her, gentle sleep,
Deep in bliss her spirit steep.

There the prisoner in his cell,
Heedless of the warning bell,
Bidding him for death prepare,
Ere he climb the fatal stair,
Laughs again, a happy child,
By no shameful sin defiled.

There the sufferer, who hath known
Throbbing brow and aching bone,
Thro' the long night's weary hours,
Feels at last his wearied powers
Gradually their force resign,
Nature's gentlest anodyne!

There the dying sometimes lie
As they near eternity;
Gently in thine arms they glide
Over death's mysterious tide;
Pass its waters chill and dark,
As within a sheltering ark.

Even so, thou gentle Sleep,
Bear me o'er the unfathomed deep;
Let no dread delusion come
O'er my spirit in the gloom;
Exorcise each form unblest,
Till I know the dreamless rest.

To C. C. R.

WHAT a world of feeling lies
　　Sleeping, Baby, in thine eyes!
Latent there, the hope and joy
Buoyant in the laughing boy:
Latent there the pride and power
Of the man's maturer hour:
And, ah me! if founts of woe
Deeply lie concealed below—
If earth's passion, sin, and care,
　　Must their limpid beauty stain,
In His Heaven, God grant they wear
　　Infant innocence again.

June, 1873.

They have not needed to be purified;
　For God, beyond our earthly wisdom wise,
Has closed them here that they may open wide,
　Where nothing can defile—in Paradise.

Feb., 1879.

Waiting.

FROM THE FRENCH OF VICTOR HUGO.

CLIMB, Squirrel, climb the oak-tree high;
    Up yon light branch so near the sky
  Leap, while it quivers like a reed!
Stork, to the ancient towers true,
Cleave with strong wing the ether blue,
From church to citadel pursue
    Thy flight, from spire to turret speed!

Old Eagle, from thine eyrie rise,
Up to the mountain-top, where lies
  Eternal winter's stainless snow!
And thou, low-couched on dewy lawn,
Restless to spring and greet the dawn,
Which never has thy chant foregone,
    Blithe Lark! to heaven on swift wing go!

And now, from height of forest oak,
From pinnacle of marble look,
   From snowy hill, from fiery dome :
Upon the horizon's misty air
Mark ye a feather floating fair,
A panting steed whose paces bear
   My Love to my embraces home ?

A Funeral.

FROM THE GERMAN OF GRUPPE.

NIGHT passes—dawn's first red is gleaming
   From Heaven's bright edge across the hill,
And yet the bird, his small head dreaming,
   'Twixt wing and bosom hideth still.

But voices sing—low, clear—I listen
   Till on the lake the sound has died ;
Now in the cloister tapers glisten ;
   Thro' fleecy snow the sisters glide.

Silent, they form a scant procession ;
   Death thinneth fast their convent-home ;
Yestreen he claimed a fair possession—
   They bear their youngest to the tomb.

A few low prayers the women mutter ;
   No tear is shed of anguish wild ;
No sobs a spirit's anguish utter ;
   Nor desolate man stands there, nor child.

Still fall the tender flakes, and smother
   The grave, till not one clod is seen ;
Silence reigns far and wide—another
   Day breaks, as no strange thing had been.

The Duty of Man.

FROM THE FRENCH.

WITH seeming dignity, but pride in sooth,
    The Roman Judge demanded, "What is Truth?"
The Man-Divine, wise to confound or teach,
Vouchsafed no answer to the haughty speech.
Still doth that silence eloquently speak:
Truth is not ours to claim, tho' much we seek;
For, when one day a simple citizen
Saluted Jesus in the street, and then
Sought, with a wise solicitude, to learn
What might man's duty and estate concern
On this great theme, affecting all mankind,
He, the Omniscient, spake the Eternal mind,
Proclaiming in one word His high decree—
" Love God, and love thy fellows," answered He :
This man's sufficing law—from Heaven above
He has learned all when he has learned to love.

Lines Written in a Ronsard.

FROM THE FRENCH OF COPPÉE.

TOLEDO ruled in her old days of fame
    That, ere the prentice armourer might bear
The workman's title, sleep he must forswear
To watch one night beside the furnace flame :
Then toil a masterpiece of steel to frame
Supple and strong, and light as plume in air,

Hot from the anvil take the sword, and there
Inscribe in gratitude his master's name.
Thus, Ronsard, I with thee my vigil passed,
Thus, with a pupil's lowly faith essayed
Thy swordlike sonnet, flexible and strong:
'Neath my sonorous hammer sounded long
The metal, rosy from the forge's blast,
And thy great name I graved upon the blade.

The Little Shroud.

FROM THE GERMAN.

THE little Child was dead: the Mother gave
    Her spirit up to unrestrained regret;
Thro' the long day she wept, and at sunset,
Still weeping, sate beside her Darling's grave:
Then at her side she saw him stand: "I crave
One boon," he said, "sweet Mother: see, so wet
Thy tears have made my shroud that I as yet
Nor rest nor slumber know in earth's still cave.
Oh rest thee!" Soft he vanished, and she rose;
And now she goes about her household ways
And sheds no tear, only a sad smile plays
Upon her quivering lips, for well she knows,
While she to patience soothes her swelling breast,
The little shroud is dry, her child at rest.

"Tempus Fugit."

FROM THE GERMAN OF LEBRECHT DREVES.

GUST unto gust thro' the forest is calling,
   Southward already the little birds start,
Sweetheart! how soon are the summer leaves falling!
   Sweetheart! how soon must all beauty depart!

Scarce has the hawthorn unfolded its blossom;
   Scarce has the rose shaped her fair buds of May;
Scarce has Love's rapture o'erbrimmed the fond bosom,
   When the leaves fall, and all passeth away.

Love that now yearneth, now sootheth, now paineth,
   Like a brief fading dream hasteneth by.
When the day endeth, O then what remaineth?
   We have no answer, Dear, only a sigh.

Still where the rose with her sweet ashes covers
   The earth, yet another next summer shall bloom;
Soon with fond kisses will happy young lovers
   Plight a new troth o'er the moss on our tomb.

A Last Wish.

FROM THE FRENCH OF SULLY PRUD'HOMME.

YE who would aid me in mine agony,
   Stand silent by:
Let me but hear one tender harmony,
   Content I die.

Bid music lull, enchant me, and undo
   Earth's heavy chain:
Rock pain to rest, but, I entreat of you,
   From speech refrain.

Sick am I of men's words, they swerve and bend,
    And truth conceal;
More dear the sounds I may not comprehend,
    But only feel.

Bring melody my parting soul to bear
    On its light breath,
From her delirium into dreamland fair,
    From thence, to death.

Listen, Madelaine.

FROM THE FRENCH OF VICTOR HUGO.

LISTEN, listen, Madelaine,
    Winter leaves at last the plain
  Frozen only yestermorn;
'Neath these drooping branches come,
Far afield my pages roam,
  Tempted by a wandering horn.

I could fancy, Madelaine,
That the spring, whose breath again
  Paints the roses of thy bowers,
Shook last night, to pleasure thee,
From her flowing drapery,
  All this wondrous wealth of flowers.

I could envy, Madelaine,
That white lamb who lent the skein
  Woven by those fingers small:
Or yon little bird in air,
Softly fluttering here and there,
  Answering thy gentle call.

I am jealous, Madelaine,
Of the Priest of Tombelaine,
   When in grave confessional,
To his ear thy lips betray
Little sins of yesterday,
   Soft avowals virginal.

I would linger, Madelaine
'Neath thy chamber's latticed pane,
   When the pale night-butterfly
With his bold wing tapping there,
Whiles thou dost for rest prepare,
   Startles thy sweet privacy.

When thy bosom, Madelaine,
Doth its nightly freedom gain
   From its vesture's close embrace,
And, lest those shy eyes should see
Thine own shrinking purity,
   Thou dost veil thy mirror's face!

An it please thee, Madelaine,
Thy proud dwelling shall contain
   Vassals, squires, and pages fair,
And thy splendid oratory
Shall 'neath richest tapestry
   Hide its marble arches rare.

An it please thee, Madelaine,
For the spray of marjolaine
   Now entwined amidst thy curls,
That fair brow a crown shall bear,
Such as titled ladies wear,
   All embossed with shimmering pearls.

An it please thee, Madelaine,
Lady of the Land to reign
　　With a knight of high degree,
Quit for him thy lowly cot,
Or, if this thou wouldest not,
　　Bid him shepherd turn for thee.

Her Name.

FROM THE FRENCH OF VICTOR HUGO.

THE lily's scent, the aureole's misty ray,
　　Day's latest murmur light,
Pity of friends, whose tears their solace say,
The strange farewells of time, the whispering play
　　When lovers' lips unite.

The seven-hued banner in the sky displayed,
　　Left by the storm a trophy to the sun,
A voice beloved we deemed in silence laid,
The tenderest promise of a tender maid,
　　Of dreams, life's earliest one.

The chant of distant choir, the sigh at dawn,
　　From fabled Memnon's lips,
The softest sound that trembles, and is gone,
The sweetest thought from fancy's chambers drawn,
　　Her Name doth all eclipse.

Let it be spoken low, even as a prayer,
　　Be ever of my hymns the soft refrain,
The hidden lamp lighting a temple fair,
The word which echoes thro' its depths of air,
　　Again and yet again.

O Friends, before my muse, with speech of flame,
    Soaring in realms forbidden,
Dare link with names profane pride would proclaim
That my soul's love hath kept her stainless name
    As holy treasure hidden;

The hymns which to her lyre my spirit sings
    Shall rise from bended knees—a Litany,
Till the soft air, stirred by the quiverings strings,
Shall seem responsive to the unseen wings
    Of Angels passing by.

"Universal Liberty."

FROM THE FRENCH OF PIERRE DUPONT.

WE, for whom the lamp of morning
    At the cock-crow sheds its ray,
Who, for doubtful guerdon toiling,
    At the forge prevent the day;
Who, with every limb, nerve, muscle,
    In unceasing work engage,
Not to win a prosperous morrow,
    But to escape a beggared age:
      Let us strength in union see;
      Let us drink in harmony;
      Whatsoever message come
      From the cannon, hoarse or dumb,
      Let us drink—the toast shall be,
        Universal Liberty!

With a grasp relaxing never,
    From harsh soil and jealous wave,
Wrest we stores of hidden treasure,
    Dainty food and raiment brave,

Pearls, and diamonds, and metals,
   Hill-side fruits, the valley's sheaves;
Hapless sheep! what costly mantles
   Of our wool the tyrant weaves!
     Let us strength, &c.

What gain we by bearing burdens,
   'Neath whose weight we feebly bend?
What, by shedding sweat of labour?
   Like machines our lives we spend!
Lo! our Babels mount to Heaven!
   Earth from us her wealth derives;
When the bees have wrought the honey
   They are driven from the hives!
     Let us strength, &c.

Clad in rags and housed in hovels,
   'Midst rude heaps of refuse laid;
Like to owls we seek the darkness;
   Like to thieves we hide in shade:
Still our blood with life is ruddy,
   Still tumultuously it flows;
We would revel in the sunlight,
   Underneath the oak's green boughs!
     Let us strength, &c.

Whensoe'er across our country
   Streams of blood flow broad and deep,
Their red waves but water harvests
   Which the hands of tyrants reap:
Guard we from like loss the future;
   Love is stronger far than hate!
Some glad breeze from Earth or Heaven
   Must blow at last—and, while we wait,
     Let us strength, &c.

The Saw-Mill.

FROM THE GERMAN OF KÖRNER.

MY heart for rest was yearning,
   I sate the mill beside,
I watched the swift wheel turning,
   I watched the waters glide.

I watched with senses dreaming,
   The smooth saw's pliant length
Into the pine-wood gleaming
   Plunge in its cruel strength,

The slender pine tree shivered,
   As fraught with sentient life,
While every fibre quivered,
   With mournful music rife.

It sang, "Thy steps have wandered
   At fitting moment here;
For thee my life is squandered,
   For thee fierce wounds I bear".

"Though onward still thou'rt faring,
   A shrine of quiet rest
Is from my wood preparing
   For thee on earth's soft breast".

Four planks fell down—the clamour
   Roused me—my heart was chill:
Ere I one word could stammer
   The busy wheel was still.

The Fay.

FROM THE FRENCH OF VICTOR HUGO.

IS she Morgane, or Urgèle?
   I know not—in dreams divine
Comes a Fay, transparent, frail,
And she droops her forehead pale,
   Flower-like, till it touches mine.

Your weird ballads, bards of old,
   She on ivory lute repeats:
Slight my faith in tales ye told,
Had ye not, O singers bold!
   More than matched your heroes' feats.

She commands that I revere,
   And uphold the true and right;
That at once my hand severe
Strike the harp of a trouvère,
   Wear the gauntlet of a knight.

Do I to the wilds depart
   She lies hid 'neath all around,
Making, for my poet-heart,
From each ray a glory start,
   Voices speak in every sound.

When my hearth in winter glows,
   She unto my feet doth creep,
Points me to the skies, and shows
Stars that close, and shine, and close,
   Like fair eyes o'erpowered with sleep.

She, the shades of forests hoar
   Peoples with primeval man ;
Shadows flit mine eyes before,
'Neath the trees' dark arches roar
   Torrents born when Time began.

When at night a watch I keep,
   She from vexing fancies leads,
And, to soothe mine ear to sleep,
Wakes, in realms of silence deep,
   Music as of shepherds' reeds.

Is she Morgane, or Urgèle ?
   I know not—in dreams divine,
With transparent form, and frail,
Comes a Fay, whose forehead pale,
   Flower-like droops, and touches mine.

Moses on the Nile.

FROM THE FRENCH OF VICTOR HUGO.

"COME, sisters, fresh the wave at break of day,
   Come, the tired reaper sleeps the morn away,
     And all the shore is free :
From drowsy Memphis still no murmur flows,
And our chaste sports beneath these shading boughs
     Only the dawn may see.

" My father's courts Art's choicest treasures hold ;
But, fairer than their porphyry or gold,
     I deem this bank's wild wreath :
The songs I love are warbled in the sky,
And, sweeter than all scents of Araby,
     Is this soft zephyr's breath.

"Come, for the wave is calm, the sky is pure;
Leave here your azure robes to float secure;
    There let your girdles rest:
Help me to cast my crown and veil aside,
For I to-day must frolic on the tide,
    The great Nile's heaving breast.

"Haste! linger not!—but thro' the mist of morn
What see I there, along the river borne?
    Look not so timidly!
Some ancient palm-tree carried by the tide,
Leaving his deserts for the ocean wide,
    Our pyramids would see.

"What have I said? if I may trust my sight,
'Tis Hermes' bark, or shell of Isis white,
    Riding the light wave's crest:
Nay! 'tis a cradle, and in placid sleep,
A tender infant lies upon the deep,
    As on a mother's breast.

"He sleeps, and from afar his floating bed
Seems, as it rocks, by wind and wave bestead,
    The nest of some fair dove:
It wanders on, all at their fitful will
Tossed to and fro, but yet he slumbers still,
    Cradled his grave above.

"He wakes! O Maids of Memphis, hasten, run!
He weeps! What mother thus could leave her son
    To drift 'midst tangled weeds?
He spreads his little arms:—the waters purr
About him, and they have no barrier
    Save that frail fence of reeds.

" Save him !—methinks some Hebrew child we see
My father has proscribed : how cruel he,
    With innocence at strife !
O feeble babe ! maternal feelings glow
Within this heart for thee, and thou shalt owe
    To me, not birth, but life ! "

Thus Iphis spoke, hope of a monarch dread,
As by the Nile her gentle troop she led,
    Wandering all carelessly :
Fair were her maids, but all their beauty paled
When she, ' The daughter of the Kings,' unveiled,
    Seemed ' Daughter of the Sea !'

Now froths the wave about her shrinking feet :
Trembling she moves—impelled by pity sweet—
    Towards the infant's side.
She lifts the cot, charmed with her tender load,
As ne'er before upon her forehead broad
    Blend modesty and pride.

Soon thro' the tide, treading the rushes low,
She bears the rescued babe with footsteps slow,
    And on the shore doth lay :
Then, turn by turn, her maidens bending, place
Their timid kisses on his rosy face,
    Smiling his fears away.

" Fond mother, gazing from afar, draw nigh,
Thine infant, watched by Heaven's own gracious eye,
    Again thine arms shall know.
Fear nought ; the secret of thine happiness,
Iphis, not yet a Mother, may not guess,
    So let the glad tears flow."

Now, while the Princess, with her joyful throng,
To the stern Pharaoh bears the babe along,
    On high the Angel Choirs
Their legions filling all the starry sky,
Their faces veiled before God's Majesty,
    Sing to the eternal lyres.

" Mourn not, O Jacob ! cease to blend thy tears
With Nile's dark flood ; spread in thy sight appears
    The Jordan's fertile shore :
Swift comes the happy hour when Goshen yields
Her captives up, to seek the promised fields,
    Captives at last no more.

" See, in yon babe borne up the watery strand,
The Elect of Sinai, by whose strong hand
    God's judgments shall be hurled.
Vain Mortals, who presume His ways to tell,
Kneel! Thro' a cradle saves He Israel ;
    So will He save the world ! "

Summer Rain.

FROM THE FRENCH OF VICTOR HUGO.

COME out, the eve is fresh and sweet,
    For showers fell at morn ;
Let wet grass bathe thy slender feet,
    Its green their white adorn :
The small bird flutters thro' the brakes,
The moisture from his wings he shakes,
    Poor bird, by Heaven blest !
Singing, he hears the wind sweep by,
Singing, he sees bright raindrops lie
    Like pearls within his nest.

The clouds their precious stores have shed,
  Skies take again their blue ;
The fields shine, newly waterèd,
  A silvery network through ;
The swollen streamlet of the plain
Drags bordering grasses in its train,
  And lizards, sleeping caught :
It hurries on, and downward slants,
Leaping the stones, till, for the ants,
  Niagaras are wrought.

And, whirling in the deluge swift,
  See oarlesss insects glide,
Seizing the frailest rafts, they drift
  On gnat-wings down the tide ;
And some to leaves like islands cling,
Asylums small and wandering,
  Yet joy their woes will crown,
If but one little straw there is
Upon the brink of the abyss,
  To stay their floating town.

In the warm sunshine vapours rise
  From all the watery plain ;
The tremulous horizon flies,
  Glimmers, and flies again ;
See how, 'neath shadowy veils there lie,
Like stars that gleam uncertainly,
  Points sparkling luminous ;
And mountains shine thro' flying mist,
And roofs that stream with rain are kissed
  By sunlight glorious.

O'er the moist meadows we may stray
  Alone at this sweet time ;
Shyly in mine thy soft arm lay,
  And come where yonder lime

Spreads its cool shade; the sun sinks fast,
But, ere thou watch him smile his last,
   Look for a moment back,
Where palace and where cottage knows
One radiance, and the city glows
   Golden on skies of black.

And see, how fast the smoke-wreaths glide
   O'er roofs where mists still brood;
There—glad wives in true love confide,
   There—rest sad souls subdued:
Through life, which some to leave are fain,
The sun still follows after rain,
   And shines behind the showers;
The windows of the city glow
Bathed in his fires, and flaming show
   Like eyes, 'neath brows of towers.

There is the rainbow! clear its span
   Is rounded on the sky!
What treasures God still keeps for man
   When storms have past him by!
How oft, ye spheres thro' space that roll,
Has, for his wings, my longing soul,
   With some Ithuriel striven,
Just to discover whither tends
That mighty curve that downward bends—
   Arch of a bridge of Heaven!

The Young Mother.

TRANSLATED FROM THE GERMAN OF JULIUS STURM.

THE Baby weeps—on pillows white
   The Mother lays her Darling tender,
But he, by tears o'erpowered quite,
   Will not to rest or sleep surrender.

To soothe his woes, tune after tune,
   Soft, and more soft, the Mother singeth,
And round the little cradle soon
   Slumber its fairy girdle flingeth.

And ever, as the music sinks,
   Faint, and more faint, grows Baby's crying,
Till on his closed eye's quivering brinks,
   Teardrops unshed are softly lying.

Then the sweet glamour of a dream
   Plays lightly o'er each baby feature;
The Mother scarce to breathe doth seem
   Brooding above the tiny creature.

With timid hand she foldeth close
   The coverlet about her treasure;
She longs to kiss his cheek, but knows
   A kiss might break that trance of pleasure.

She gazes on him, rapt in bliss,
    Leaves him awhile, but soon returning,
Eases her full heart with a kiss
    For which her very lips are yearning.

Then, with a sigh of grateful joy,
    Beside the little bed she kneeleth,
Asks Heaven's best blessing on her boy,
    And to her own rest softly stealeth.

For the Day of Intercession for Missions.

LET one sound of supplication
   From the Church's heart arise,
All her earthly temples filling,
   Let it pierce the lofty skies;
Till it reach the courts of Heaven,
   Till it gain God's gracious ear,
And by faith and love prevailing
   Heavenly blessings earthward bear.

Not for worldly gifts beseech we,
   Not for power or wealth or fame,
But that through His fair creation
   God will glorify His Name;
That true hearts by Him inspired
   May with holy fervour glow,
Ready o'er the waste of waters
   With His olive-branch to go.

Could we feel the silent yearning
   Of the heathen for his God,
See the hopeless void before him
   When his life's dark path is trod,
Mark the vain oblations offered
   At the helpless idol's knee,
If perchance some hope of blessing
   For his weary soul might be,—

Every heart would swell with pity,
   Every hand would haste to give
Freely of its richest treasure
   That the dying soul might live:
And the young, the brave, the happy
   Would rejoice to spread abroad
Tidings of a great salvation
   Through the lands that know not God.

O Thou Universal Father,
   Hear thy happier children's prayer;
In the blessings of Thine Advent
   May the heathen nations share.
Give the seed and guide the sower,
   Where in zealous faith he goes,
Till the wilderness rejoicing
   Bud and blossom as the rose.

Now to Thee, Almighty Father,
   With Thine own Adored Son,
And the Spirit Pure and Holy,—
   One in Three and Three in One—
Thanks for blesings past we offer,
   Prayer for blessings yet to be,
Glory in the Highest yielding
   Now and evermore to Thee.—Amen.

For a Vigil.*

FOR all thy Saints, O Lord, whose quiet slumber
  Is guarded by the gates of Paradise—
That blessed multitude no tongue may number
  Who peaceful wait till Christ shall bid arise—
We bless Thy Name, and thank Thee, Lord, that they
Found strength on earth to tread Thy narrow way.

Yea, in this quiet vigil hour we tender
  Our praise to Thee for every grace they showed ;
For their firm faith, their holy self-surrender ;
  The fervent love which in their bosoms glowed :
For these, for all, we bless Thee, O our God,
And long to follow in the path they trod.

Down Time's long vista, from the world's creation,
  We see them stream, a great, a glorious band ;
Prophets and Patriarchs of Thy favoured nation
  Lead the long line from every race and land,
Still lengthening, widening, till the gathering bright
Receives the Saints who pass from earth to-night.

And now they rest, all pain, all trial over,
  No weary watch their happy spirits keep ;
Theirs the calm home, whose hallowed shades did cover
  Three days their Saviour's Soul in mystery deep :
And we, who, waiting still on earth remain,
Would watch and pray that perfect rest to gain.

---

* Written by request to suit the beautiful tunes in *Hymns Ancient and Modern*, to F. W. Faber's "Hark! Hark! my Soul."

Like them, O Lord, we will not shrink from sorrow
   Thy love ordains to bring us nearer Thee ;
So we with them may hail that glorious morrow,
   Whose morn shall break when all the shadows flee,
Where, beyond Paradise—more blessed still—
Are light and life, upon Thy Holy Hill.   Amen.

Dedication of a Church.

O GOD Whose glorious Presence fills
   All space of earth and sea ;
Thy Throne the everlasting hills,
   The sky its canopy,
How should the creatures of Thine Hand
   Build Thee, O Lord, a Shrine,
When Nature's fanes in every land
   Are Thine, and only Thine ?

Great Architect of matchless skill,
   Our highest aim above ;
Well might we tremble and be still,
   Did we not trust Thy Love ;
On this relying, now we dare
   To dedicate to Thee
This House, for holy praise and prayer,
   Unworthy though it be.

Lord, by Thy grace the fabric stands,
   For Thou, the labour wrought
By loving hearts and skilful hands,
   Hast blessed beyond our thought.
Fair seems it in our sight we own,
   May it be fair in Thine,
Adorned by many a living stone
   Of the great Church divine.

That holy Church, Thy Spirit's power
  To perfect grace shall mould,
Then, when the temples of an hour
  Sink in oblivion cold,
On the eternal Rock secure,
  And with Its strength endowed,
It shall through endless years endure,
  Thy Dwelling-place, O God.—Amen.

Sursum Corda.

LINES SUGGESTED BY THE DEDICATION OF A CHAPEL,

September 1st, 1880.

O THE heavenly City fair!
  When we muse upon its grace,
When the glory we compare
  Of that high and holy place,
With the best our art designs,
  With the best our skill achieves,
Then the humbled heart resigns
  Every thought that pride conceives.

When our fancy ranging far,
  Far beyond these veiling skies,
Sees more bright than any star
  Light that lightens Paradise;
Then how low the roof we rear!
  Then how dim our storied panes!
Then how small, how dark appear
  Even the fairest earthly fanes!

When to the entrancèd ear
  Hosts of radiant angels sing,
And from heaven's distant sphere
  Wide their mystic numbers fling;

Then how faint the songs of earth,
   Though they rise from sweetest choirs,
Though the lips that give them birth
   Love attunes and hope inspires!

Yet our best we offer Thee;
   Lord, accept it, and forgive,
And vouchsafe at last that we
   May with perfect powers perceive
Beauty only dreamed below,
   Harmony to earth denied,
Where the highest hopes we know
   Shall, in Thee, be satisfied. Amen.

For Easter Eve, after Confirmation.

"Before the Morning Watch."

IN this calm Eve, before the Easter morn—
   That morn which soon our longing eyes shall see—
We in Christ's temple stand, His soldiers sworn,
   With Him to rise and share His victory.

Even so of old the chosen knight would stand,
   So keeping vigil watch the eastern skies,
Ready, his virgin mail and sword at hand,
   To rise and wear his warrior dignities.

Our night is well nigh past, the solemn time
   Of contrite prayer and penitential tears;
Up the dim East ere long the morn will climb,
   And hope and gladness triumph over fears.

Soon will the grave disclose its mysteries;
   Soon will the sealèd stone be rolled away
By angel hands: soon will our Lord arise—
   The Sun that shineth to the perfect day.

To-morrow we the Paschal Feast shall keep,
  And at His Table meet our risen King;
O thither may we haste with reverence deep
  The first-fruits of our happy youth to bring!

The faith of soldiers armèd for His war,
  The love of children made indeed His own;
O Blessed Saviour, all we have and are
  We there would consecrate to Thee alone.—Amen.

Thanksgiving for Deliverance from Sickness.

"Unto God the Lord belong the issues from death."—Ps. lxviii. 20.

FATHER, All-wise, All-good,
  Once more Thy children meet,
With health and strength alike renewed,
  To worship at Thy feet.
They come to pour their praise
  For every gift restored;
To own that life and length of days
  Are blessings from the Lord.

Saviour, whose human arm
  Oft rose to cure and bless,
Whose earthly Presence bore a charm
  Against all earth's distress,
We thank Thee that Thy touch
  From Heaven is still the same;
That to the sick and sorrowing couch
  Its balm of healing came.

Most Holy Comforter,
  Spirit Divine, to Thee
With equal love we praise prefer,
  And lowly bend the knee:
Deigning Thy gracious art
  Of solace to employ,
Thou, Lord, hast bid the anxious heart
  To sing aloud for joy.

Throughout this mortal race
  Until we reach its goal,
Great Trinity of Might, Love, Grace,
  Still keep us, heal, console;
And grant that they who late
  Rose from Thy chastening rod
May own the Hand that ruled their fate,
  And love their loving God.

[And if some drops of gall
  Mix with our chalice sweet,
The blended draught is blest for all
  Who drink it at Thy feet.
Lord, both of life and death,
  For our dear brother gone
We thank Thee, though with faltering breath,
  And say, "Thy will be done."]

To Thy great name a strain
  Of praise and love be poured
By those who yet on earth remain—
  Those who are with their Lord.
And when the closing night
  Of Earth's brief day shall come,
Great Trinity of Grace, Love, Might,
  Take all for ever Home.—Amen.

Trinity, 1875.

Harvest Hymn.

"First the blade, then the ear, after that the full corn in the ear."

LO! the golden spoil we gather
   In a silent language tells
Of Thy love, Almighty Father,
   Which all other love excels ;
Thou, with bounty undeserved
   By the creatures of Thy hand,
Hast another year preserved
   Peace and plenty in our land.

Late the sower where he laid it,
   Left in faith the scattered seed,
Left it where His eye Who made it
   Might alone its nurture heed ;
Soon the slender blades were showing
   Through rough soil their vernal green,
Now a golden harvest glowing
   Floods with light the autumnal scene.

Lord, we bring with grateful pleasure
   Unto Thee our thanks and praise,
Consecrate to Thee the leisure
   Of our happy festal days :
We have watched the reaper bending
   Low beneath the August sun,
Now we see the joyful ending
   Of the work in faith begun.

Thine were all the silent powers
   That have made Thy gift complete,
Thine the softening springtide showers,
   Thine the ripening summer heat :

Blight and mildew Thou hast stayed
   By Thy strong compelling will,
Storm and tempest have obeyed,
   Thunders at Thy voice been still.

Lord, to Thee with grateful pleasure
   Bring we now our thanks and praise,
While of all the lavish treasure
   That with plenty fills our days,
We would give with hand unsparing,
   Want and sorrow to relieve,
One another's burdens bearing,
   Freely give as we receive.

And may every harvest granted,
   To our thoughtful spirits show
How Thy seed within them planted
   Unto perfect grain should grow;
O, may that great final reaping,
   Which for wheat and tares must come,
See us in angelic keeping
   Borne to Heavenly Garners home!   Amen.

www.ingramcontent.com/pod-product-compliance
Lightning Source LLC
Chambersburg PA
CBHW020154170426
43199CB00010B/1037